DIAMON

THE LIFE AND DEATH OF JAYNE MANSFIELD

Veronica,

Thanks for Everything!

-Frank F.

FRANK FERRUCCIO

Outskirts Press, Inc.
Denver, Colorado

Outskirts Press
http://www.outskirtspress.com

ISBN-13: 978-1-4327-1241-9

Library of Congress Control Number: 2001012345

Outskirts Press and the "OP" logo are trademarks belonging to
Outskirts Press, Inc.

Printed in the United States of America

I dedicate this book to My Mother, who has always been there to support me, as well as my Partner John, who has endured and embraced my unconditional love of Jayne Mansfield.

TABLE OF CONTENTS

FOREWORD

The reason that I am writing this book is simply my love and adoration for the late great Actress Jayne Mansfield. People always ask me why my interest in Jayne, and this is my story.

My parents had me when they were in their early forties, my sister was 16, my brother 10. By the time I was 8 years old, my sister had left home to marry, my brother started college out of state, which basically left me an only child. Since my Father was the sole income of the household, he worked a lot to pay my brothers college tuition, and support my mother and myself. I didn't have a lot of friends, which left a lot of time for me to spend alone or with my mother, who because of, I developed a serious love for classic cinema. At the time, my favorite actress was Marilyn Monroe, I thought that she was very beautiful, and a very complex actress.

Being one of the first in the late 1970's to be lucky enough to own one of the first 900 pound Betamax VCR players, I taped many old movies, and would scan the TV Guide weekly, to see if any of Marilyn's movies were on. As my fan adoration for Marilyn increased, I would consistently see the name, "Jayne Mansfield", in print comparing her to Monroe, only consistently belittling her. Jayne Mansfield was considered to be a budget imitation of Monroe, with bigger breasts, but much less talent. Of course being a fan of Monroe, I was naturally inclined to believe this, but was open minded to find out more about her. Around the time of my curiosity in Jayne Mansfield peaking, a 1980 TV-Movie of the week premiered, staring another favorite blonde from one of my favorite TV shows, WKRP in Cincinnati, actress Loni Anderson. As I watched the movie, which was poorly based on fact about Jayne, but warmly portrayed by Anderson, I began to see that there was a lot more to this actress, than her obvious physical attributes.

After this I became obsessed with finding out more about Jayne, which was a fairly difficult task in the early nineteen eighties, long before the age of internet and computers. I called around to many different libraries in the area, and found one that had an out of print biography of the late actress in their stock. I made my father drive me three towns away so I could join as an out of town member and check out the book. It was called, "Jayne Mansfield and the American Fifties" by Martha Saxton. It was a very easy read, filled with facts not fiction, portraying Jayne as a feminist in very non-feminist time, a single working mother, who loved her five children, but wouldn't miss a move to maintain or forward in her career. It was a very warm, sympathetic look at Jayne, and about her being a victim of the time, and of much prejudice.

After reading about her being buried in a small cemetery with her family, in a small town called Pen Argyl, Pennsylvania, I made my brother take me to it, since we were only about a little over an hour away. Jayne has the biggest heart shaped headstone in the main part of Fairview Cemetery, and is by far, the star attraction.

Knowing that her children all lived out west in California, I felt bad that the grave had no flowers at all at it, so I took it upon myself to make it my commitment, to take care of her final resting place. I always make sure that she has flowers in the spring around her birthday April 19th, I will bring a pink rose tribute on June 29th, the anniversary of her passing, and I will always bring a large pink decorated grave blanket around the holidays.

I have done this since I was 13 years old, and that is just over 27 years that I have faithfully done this. It is because of this that I have met many members of Jayne's family, including her two ex-husbands, and all five of her wonderful children.

I co-own, one of the best sites on the internet about her, jaynemansfield.net which was founded by another devotee of Jayne, Kim Rosenthal. Kim started a site for Jayne online on the internet before there were any, and has maintained in all the years without any help out of her love in memory for Jayne. With the help of my personally owned pictures, and the amazing web graphics of Damien Santrioni, another huge fan of Jayne, we are I feel confident, the nicest tribute on the internet.

Jayne Mansfield fans are very different than Marilyn fans, I feel that we are all committed to preserving and enhancing Jayne's memory, and we accept Jayne through her faults and humanity for all. Jayne's biggest fan, Hillary, changed her last name to Mansfield, she is the most devoted to Jayne Patticatt a.k.a. Patti Ivy, a very beautiful and sexy natural platinum headed blonde, exudes the look of what Mansfield would have become if she had lived. She is sexy, talented and a great mother and grandmother, just as Jayne was.

We have regular fan club meetings in Pen Argyl, and at my home in New Jersey, where I store the largest personally owned Jayne Mansfield Item collection in the world.

I really am writing this because I feel there is not enough literary material on Jayne, and there has not been a major book written about her in the past fifteen years. With Jayne's youngest daughter, Mariska Hargitay, such a huge personality and extremely talented award winning actress, there has been much renewed interest in Jayne and I feel it is time to the story to be told in it's truest form.

I do not wish to upset anyone by writing this, these are my views, my knowledge and feel there hasn't been a factual life story of Jayne told. I feel very fortunate to have been embraced by the Family of Jayne Mansfield, and told many stories and facts first hand by the people who knew her better than anyone, her family. I just hope that I can do her story justice, so lets get on with the incredible story of her life.

CHAPTER ONE
IN THE BEGINNING

Jayne Mansfield was born Vera-Jayne Palmer on April 19, 1933 in the small town of Phillipsburg, New Jersey. Her parents Herbert & Vera Palmer anxiously awaited the birth of their only child, and little "Jaynie", as her parents called her, soon became the apple of her fathers eye.

When Jayne was only three her father, Herbert Palmer, suffered a massive heart attack while they were taking a Sunday drive, swerving off the road, and pronounced dead at the scene. Her mother, Vera, took Jayne back across the Delaware River to a small town where Vera was born & raised in Pen Argyl, Pennsylvania. Vera & Jayne were surrounded by lots of family, both the late Herbert Palmer's parents, as well as Vera's, lived in Pen Argyl, along with Helen & Bert Milheim, Vera's close sister and brother-in-law, and their children, Richard, Cynthia & Doug.

Cynthia, Jayne first cousin, was her closest family member to Jayne's heart, they stayed the best and closest, Jayne's whole life.

When the kids were just around 5 years old, Vera's sister Helen was awoken in the middle of the night, by Vera, ranting how little Jaynie wasn't in her bed, when Helen looked in on her children, they were also missing. The two sisters were filled with fear as they called the local police, stating their children had been kidnapped.

About an hour after the police were alerted, the children were located in Weonia Park, which was about a half a mile away from the house. Jayne wanted to play on the swings, and woke up her cousins for them all to sneak out with her, even as a child, Jayne was the star of the town.

Vera taught in elementary school in Pen Argyl and Jayne grew older around several first & second cousins. Vera met a very nice man soon after named Harry Peers, and their relationship progressed quickly into a marriage. Jayne was fond of her stepfather, but always felt sad about losing her father who she remembered dearly.

When Jayne was just 6 years old, Harry & Vera Peers packed up and moved to Dallas, Texas, where Harry had been transferred to. Vera enrolled her baby Jayne into numerous dance and musical programs, Jayne was taught Piano as well as violin. Vera was determined to see her baby become successful in some kind of art, a frustrated dream that Vera was never able to achieve herself.

Jayne excelled in piano & violin and had many musical solo performances in school recitals, as well as dance. Jayne at a very early age had a powerful fascination with the movies. Where most children have their rooms filled with pictures of cartoon characters, Jayne's walls were filled with rows of Glossy 8 x 10's of glamorous movie stars. Every chance Jayne got, she would dress in her mothers clothing and make-up.

Jayne developed into a stunningly well developed girl at an early age, which captured the attention of many boys of various ages. Jayne had a very active libido at an early age, and found herself completely boy crazy and dating by the age of 13. To no surprise, Jayne found herself in the family way at age 15. Jayne was terrified of telling her mother about her predicament, and found it impossible to hide her almost four month along pregnancy.

Vera and her sister Helen dragged Jayne to the doctor to find out if what they thought was true, and it was. Jayne had been dating a few boys from the area, but she suspected that the father was bad boy "Inky", who worked at the local filling station.

She told him about her predicament, and he told her that he wanted no part of "her" problem. Jayne had been dating an older boy named Paul Mansfield, who was very cute and very sweet. Paul was older than Jayne, and a very nice boy with good intentions, Jayne told him about her predicament, and Paul freely accepted the responsibility.

Not long after their marriage, little Jayne Marie was born on November 8, 1950. Her mother 16, her "father" 22. Paul was in the Army and both he and his new family lived on the base in Dallas, where Jayne caught the attention of every male with a heartbeat.

Jayne continued her education, taking baby Jayne-Marie in her carriage to class with her. Jayne got involved in many school and army drama productions and soon caught everyone's attention. Jayne had Paul promise her that when he was done with the army, that they would move to Los Angeles, a promise that Paul would regret, and Jayne would hold him to.

As soon as he was released in 1954, off they went, the Mansfield family of three.

Jayne, Jayne-Marie and Paul Mansfield packed all their stuff in their red Buick Convertible and headed west. Jayne was so excited because she knew it was only a matter of time before she would become a big star. Vera and Harry, were very sad to see them leave, but Vera also knew, that nothing or no one would ever be able to change Jayne's mind, once it was made.

As soon as they unpacked, Jayne made a phone call to Paramount studios, and told the receptionist that her name was Jayne Mansfield and that she was going to be their biggest star. The lady on the phone told her that they already had many big stars, but her persistence and overwhelming self confidence, won her a screen test.

Whatever opportunity or part that Jayne auditioned for, she did so with all of her energy, she knew that she would be able to win some casting directors full attention, and let it be noted that Jayne did not sleep her way to the top, she did it clearly on her drive and perseverance.

Jayne gradually lost the extra weight from having Jayne-Marie but soon noticed that mostly all of the roles she auditioned for were going to blondes. Jayne quickly took the "if you cant beat them join them" attitude, and soon dyed her brunette lochs Blonde. So the new buxom blonde set out determined to wipe the floor with Hollywood's current blonde Marilyn Monroe and all of her current imitators.

Jayne won a leading role in a b-movie called, THE FEMALE JUNGLE, she was paid $100 for her performance, but gladly would have done it for free, just to see herself on a movie screen.

Jayne caught the eye of a rising Publicity agent Bill Schrifin, who saw a great opportunity in Jayne. Together the two plotted and planned some of the most eye-catching stunts, in order to get Jayne in every periodical of that time. Jayne dressed in a skimpy 2-piece red velvet bikini trimmed in white fur, and delivered many bottles of liquor to the national press association.

One of Jayne's most elaborate stunts was when she was sent by her agent to Florida to participate in the premiere of sex-symbol Jane Russell's new movie, "UNDERWATER"(1955).

She accidentally on purpose left her bathing suit behind, and had to borrow an oh too tight red bathing suit. All eyes were on Jayne Mansfield and not on Jane Russell. For the second part of the photo shoot, Jayne squeezed herself into a red bikini, which just happened to become untied while she was swimming in the pool.

Needless to say, the only pictures being taken that day were of Mansfield, not Russell. The pictures appeared in every newspaper across the land, and caught the eye of most every studio. Warner bros were the first to jump on the opportunity and signed Jayne to a starter contract.

Paul Mansfield had quite enough, he tried to support her in her goals, but he was a man. A man of pride who didn't want to live in a woman's shadow, and decided to move back to Dallas. Jayne said go ahead, but Jayne-Marie stays here with me.

A very disgusted Paul had decided not to take a back seat to Jayne's career aspirations, and moved on. I guess in some way he thought that Jayne wouldn't be as successful as she was in winning parts and becoming a star, if anyone knew the real Jayne, they would know that nothing was going to stop her from achieving fame.

Paul was interviewed many years after Jayne's passing, he was quoted as saying, "He didn't want to be known, as Mr. Jayne Mansfield", but that always struck me as insanely proud, because after all, Mansfield was his last name.

Jayne liked the name Mansfield, and even after their divorce later on, decided to keep it. Jayne said, "I like the sound of Jayne Mansfield, it sounds like the name of a famous movie star".

CHAPTER TWO
THE WARNER YEAR

A ll of Jayne's publicity and drive won her a year contract with Warner Brothers Studios. While Jack Warner, seemed to really want her as one of his stars, I don't really think he knew what to do with her. At Warner's ,she appeared in 3 pictures for them, with only one having any substance to it. She had a small part in PETE KELLY"S BLUES (1955), appearing as a red headed cigarette girl. She had a couple lines while dancing in the feature, HELL ON FRISCO BAY(1955), but her best moment on screen for them was in "ILLEGAL"(1955)with Edward G. Robinson. In the movie she had a few scenes, dressed in some very tight outfits, but she had the opportunity to sing and win favorable notices. The part mimicked Marilyn Monroe's small part in ASPHALT JUNGLE (1949). This was the beginning of a long career of comparison between the two.

Still with Jayne's positive performance in ILLEGAL, she was dropped from her Warner contract, she was considered to be limited. This brought her much grief, she thought that she was on her way, and know she had been dumped by her first major studio, but not to worry, Jayne would not let this discourage her in anyway.

To keep her name and photos in the newspaper, she attended every supermarket opening from Los Angeles to San Francisco. She also competed in many pageants winning numerous beauty titles. A few of them consisted of Miss Photoflash, Miss Tomato, Miss firecracker, Miss Fire Prevention Week, Miss Cadillac and the list goes on. The only title Jayne ever turned down, was to be Miss Roquefort Cheese, because she said it just didn't sound right.

Jayne also agreed to be Hugh Hefner's centerfold for his February 1955 Playboy magazine spread. This would begin a long association between Playboy and Jayne, she would appear every February from 1955-1963.

From all of her publicity Jayne was offered a leading role in a B class film noir picture for an independent studio, which was later distributed by Columbia Pictures. The Movie was to be filmed on location in Philadelphia and Atlantic City, the movie was called, "THE BURGLAR". She co-starred with B-movie actor Dan Duryea, and it was actually one of Jayne's few serious roles. Her figure was downplayed and her hair was a light brown color. She received decent reviews after the movie premiered 2 years later in 1957, after her Broadway success in "Rock Hunter"

While filming in Atlantic City, Jayne received a phone call from her agent telling her about an opportunity to play the lead in a Broadway play. Jayne was intrigued, but needed a little coaxing from her agent to go for a reading. The part called for a "Monroe" type actress, and had been offered first to Rival Blonde Mamie Van Doren. Mamie didn't want to be type cast as Monroe type and passed on it. Jayne really didn't want to do Broadway, she had her sites fixed on being a big film star.

After more coaxing from her agent, she decided to give it a try. She auditioned while still on the east filming "the Burglar', she arrived an hour and a half late wearing a plain tan raincoat, when given her pages to read, she dropped the coat to the floor, revealing her outfit which consisted of a terry cloth towel.

George Axelrod, the play's writer was reluctant in casting an unknown for his star, along with the Director, but when Jayne was standing on stage in a towel, they both immediately realized they had found their star. Jayne received fair to good reviews for "Rock Hunter", but the play was sold out every night, everyone wanted to get a look at the woman who was always getting her picture in the paper, everyday all around the world.

While she was in the play, Jayne would make personal appearances at every supermarket or store opening in the tri-state area. She would usually receive around $5000 for each one, plus merchandise from that store.

Both before and after her performances Jayne would make her presence known around the city, by attending every show and eating in every restaurant. In 1955 there wasn't a single soul who didn't know who Jayne Mansfield was.

One night Jayne had decided to go to Mae West's show at The Latin Quarter, little did she know she was going to meet the man of her dreams that evening. Mickey Hargitay was a Hungarian body builder who achieved status of being Mr. Universe in 1955. He was one of the many muscle men who were background for Mae's act. Jayne took one look, and said….. "Who is that?"

The waiter came to the table to take Jayne's order and she said, "I'll have a steak and that man on the right….."

Jayne & Mickey instantly fell in love with each other, and spent every moment together from that day on, they even developed a little adagio dance, where Mickey would lift her to the ceiling so she could eat grapes from a chandelier. Mickey & Jayne were known all over New York for doing this little routine and it was expected.

When Mae West gave Mickey the ultimatum to stop seeing, "that blonde tramp" or he was fired from her show, Mickey pronounced that he loved her and was going to marry her, (as soon as her divorce from Paul was final). Mae had Mickey punched out, by one of the other musclemen in the show.

All of this press, and all of the appearances made Jayne known around the world, she was now a full fledged celebrity, and a hot property. Bill Schriffin, her agent had all kinds of movie contract offers being thrown at him. Twentieth Century Fox (Marilyn Monroe's Home Studio) was the most interested. The only problem was that Jayne had signed a run of the play contract, and with all the great box office, they didn't want to let Jayne go. Twentieth Century Fox was so determined to get Jayne, they bought the rights to the play, and closed the show, and Jayne was off to Hollywood.

CHAPTER THREE
THE FOX CONTRACT

2 0th Century Fox, I believe was really the reason that Jayne's movie career didn't take off. Fox was up in arms because their top star Marilyn Monroe, had walked out on her studio contract because she was tired of having no say in the movies she made. Marilyn in 1955 was the number 1 box office draw in the world.

The studio saw a chance at having another "Monroe" and thought that it would also teach Marilyn a lesson. They had tried this the year earlier, with leggy blonde actress Sheree North, but the public didn't see her as star material. Unfortunately I feel that Jayne was used as a key pawn, in getting Monroe to settle her contract issues with Fox.

Marilyn was very insecure, and Jayne was not at all. Marilyn was never fond of any blondes, especially ones that she felt were copying her image. Jayne was a huge threat to her because everywhere she turned, there was Jayne, ready for the photos, news stories, interviews and autograph signing, all of which Marilyn hid from.

People will always disagree with my opinion, but I don't think that there were any similarities between Marilyn & Jayne. The two were extremely different in personality, confidence, looks and talent. Marilyn was a better movie star, but a lot of this had to do with her coaching and directing. Jayne did have acting talent, it was seldom utilized, but it was there, and with the right direction, she could have been a bigger star than Monroe.

For whatever reason Jayne obtained her contract, she didn't care. The studio was was going to spend tons of money to make her as big a star as Marilyn, and Jayne was ready, willing and able. I believe that Fox never really liked Jayne, because she wasn't afraid to speak her mind, or cower to the studio head, Spyros Skouras. Jayne didn't care about Fox only her career, and they new that, so she was treated without respect.

Jayne, Jayne-Marie and Mickey were off to Hollywood (with a few dogs), and nothing was going to burst Jayne's bubble. Upon arriving in Hollywood Jayne purchased a small house in the Hollywood Hills on Wanda Park Drive, she knew that it would only be a stepping stone and wouldn't be there very long.

Her first project for Fox was to be "THE GIRL CANT HELP IT"(1956), it was a musical comedy . She was to play a gangsters girlfriend who wants to be a homemaker, but he wants her to be a huge star. Tom Ewell, Marilyn's co-star from The Seven Year Itch was her co-star, and the studio was spending thousands of dollars on Jayne's wardrobe to be designed by William Travilla.

The Girl Cant Help It was the first big budget Rock N Roll Movie of its kind, with special appearances by the biggest stars of the recording industry. Gene Vincent, Fats Domino, The Platters, Eddie Cochran, Abbey Lincoln and Julie London just to name a few. The film was a huge success, both financially and critically, and Jayne was hailed as a "Super Monroe".

The studio wanted to get her in as many movies as possible while she was waiting for "WILL SUCCESS SPOIL ROCK HUNTER?" to be ready for the screen. The original stage play had to be re-written for the screen, since it was based on making fun of the motion picture industry, so it was changed to be a satire on the Television world.

Jayne went from one film into the next, after "GIRL" she made a dramatic movie of John Steinbeck's novel, "THE WAYWARD BUS" (1957) co-starring another screen siren, Joan Collins. Jayne's part in this movie was a chance for her to show people she really could act, and she received good reviews for the film. Jayne played an ex-stripper to Joan Collins' alcoholic bus stop owner.

The movie also starred Dan Dailey, and Rick Jason. Jayne stole every scene she was in, she was very confident, acted very natural and never looked better. This was one of the few 20th Century Fox movies that Jayne actually talked in her "real" voice, and didn't coo or squeal, which she did in all of her dumb blonde roles.

With the huge success of "GIRL" and the good reviews from "BUS", they were ready to start filming, "Will Success Spoil Rock Hunter?". Mickey Hargitay was even cast in it as her on screen boyfriend. It also starred Tony Randall, Betsy Drake and Joan Blondell. The movie was another big hit for the studio and they felt confident that they had achieved their goal of having a new blonde goddess, just as they had replaced Betty Grable with Monroe.

While Jayne's star was climbing, the studio had reached an agreement with Marilyn Monroe. Marilyn received a new contract making $100, 000 per picture, with Script & Director approval, she will also be able to make movies for other studios as well as her newly formed Marilyn Monroe Productions. It was a great deal for Marilyn, the first of its kind for a female contract star, but it also meant that Jayne was no longer going to be there first priority.

Late in 1957 Jayne was cast in what many critics call, "the key mistake" in Jayne's Fox Career, "Kiss Them For Me" with Cary Grant., but even though she was billed under Cary Grant, Suzy Parker was ultimately the co-star.

The play had been a big success with actress Judy Holiday, but in the movie version all the blame for the movie not doing well was placed on Jayne. She was once again cast for the quick laugh, a pattern that was becoming too repetitious. The critics slaughtered her performance, they called her cheap, trampy and boring. This was the first Cary Grant film to bomb in a very long career, so who else could they blame, but poor Jayne.

Fox quickly saw that Jayne was not the Monroe replacement

they had hoped for, plus they didn't like the fact, that she would not listen to studio direction. Fox wanted Jayne to be a sex symbol, but with class, like Monroe had been for them.

Fox didn't want there rising sex symbol married with children, they wanted her to be seen with all of their famous male contract stars all over Hollywood. Jayne would not hurt Mickey, he had proved his love to her by dropping everything and moving with her to California.

Also they didn't want Jayne to do another pictorial for Playboy magazine, again Jayne didn't listen, which ultimately sealed her fate with Fox studios.

Late in 1957, Jayne pulled off one of her world famous publicity stunts. A party was being held at Romanoff's to welcome actress Sophia Loren to America. Jayne saw this as a great opportunity to upstage the Italian sex bomb.

Jayne had a special dress altered for the occasion, it was a very low cut spaghetti strap cocktail dress, which was very tight. The cleavage line on the dress was at the nipple line, so she wore her mink to the restaurant, and gradually made her way to Loren's table. She slipped off the coat and welcomed Sophia to America, of course Jayne wasn't even invited to this event.

When she found the opportunity to do so, she gradually was coaxing her left breast to pop out while she was standing over Sophia, posing for pictures. Much to her dismay her breast wouldn't budge, so she sat for a while next to her, and worked her dress down, bringing the cleavage line to the danger zone.

This was truly one of the most famously orchestrated publicity gags in Hollywood history, it really was just an incredible photo opportunity and Jayne knew the power in having her photos in every paper. Jayne kept looking at the photographers smiling, once Sophia had the chance to look up, she looked over at Jayne's breasts basically sitting out on the table.

The next photo is the most famous one of Jayne Mansfield to this current day. Sophia Loren was leering at Jayne's breasts while Jayne happily posed for the press. I think this picture has made it all over the world, and another which is the cover of Kenneth Angers book, Hollywood Babylon.

In this picture Jayne is leaning over smiling with her nipple totally exposed. Jayne was an original, way before the likes of Tara Reid, or Janet Jackson's Super Bowl stint. She was a very smart woman, a said IQ of 163, and she was named correctly by the press as " America's Smartest Dumb Blonde'.

This incident with Jayne didn't exactly win her over in Hollywood, other stars thought it was very distasteful, but Jayne just chalked it up to them being jealous. Jayne was a very confident woman, she didn't let talk or bad press get to her, she was quoted once as saying, " Even bad press is good press, the main thing is that you have everyone talking about you, the worst thing is when no one talks about you at all".

CHAPTER FOUR
1958

After Jayne's busy year of movie making, her divorce became final with Paul, and she was free to make plans to marry Mickey. Jayne was determined to make it the biggest pink wedding in history. Even though it was suppose to be a small private ceremony, Jayne had five thousand pink invitations dropped over downtown Los Angeles from a helicopter. It was a great opportunity for her to show the press how many people loved her besides Mickey. Mickey and Jayne exchanged vows on January 13, 1958 in Palos Verde's, California, at the stunning all glass Wayfarers Chapel. Even though only a hundred and fifty people were invited, there were hundreds of people surrounding the church hoping to catch a glimpse of Jayne in her stunning lace gown (it was used in The Girl Cant Help It).

After the wedding, Jayne decided that the Hargitay's should buy a mansion in Beverly Hills and live like a star and how she always dreamed she would. Jayne & Mickey bought a beautiful Mediterranean style house (formerly owned by Rudy Valee), for $76,000 at the corner of Sunset Blvd. & Carolwood drive, it was one of three houses on a cul de sac. It needed a lot of work, but

Mickey having been a carpenter in the younger part of his life, was ready willing and able to give Jayne all of the things that she wanted.

Mickey & Jayne did a quick four week stint in Las Vegas at the Tropicana for $35,000 a week, in order to pay for and furnish it. This was an incredible amount of money for the time, Jayne was only getting a $2500 a week salary from Fox, when she was ready and willing to work. Mickey & Jayne's nightclub act was so successful, they were held over for an additional two weeks. After the first of many Vegas gigs that they had, Mickey & Jayne were able to pay the house off in full, and actually buy furniture to fill the enormous house.

The first thing on the planning board, was to paint the palace pink, which the house was known as the pink palace, till it was torn down in the year 2000. Mickey worked day & night on the house, and even built a Jayne a heart shaped pool. It was the home of a grand movie star, exactly what she wanted.

Jayne wanted to have a large family (12 Kids) and was already pregnant just a few months after her honeymoon. Of course this was a problem at the studio, they wanted a blonde sex symbol, not a pregnant one. The studio was still upset that she married Mickey, now they had a blonde married sex bomb, who was pregnant.

Before she began to show, Jayne was sent to Europe to make her next picture, a Western, "THE SHERIFF OF FRACTURED JAW"(1958) which co-starred English actor Kenneth More. Jayne was the owner of a saloon, she rode a horse, fired a gun and sang (not really, her voice was dubbed by Connie Francis).

When the studio didn't know what to do with their "trouble" stars, they would lend them to Foreign productions. Studios made thousands of dollars while Jayne only made her regular salary of $2500 a week.

When Jayne returned from Spain, with Mickey & Jayne-Marie, the studio wanted her to rush another film, "Holiday for Lovers" with Clifton Webb & Jane Wyman. Jayne was suppose to play their eldest daughter, but when she returned home she was already gaining weight and appeared pregnant, so the part went to Carol Lynley. It didn't really matter, the film bombed anyway, and it just would have been blamed on Jayne again.

At the conclusion of 1958, Jayne gave birth to a healthy 10 pound 4 ounce boy, by C-section who Mickey and her named, Miklos on Dec 21, 1958. He had blonde hair and big blue eyes, and was named after Mickey and his father before him.

CHAPTER FIVE
BUSY IN 59

Jayne picked up a good amount of weight during her pregnancy, and it was expected for her to lose that weight and be ready to work as soon as possible. Studio "doctors" prescribed diet pills, to help her and give her energy to keep up with her schedule. Jayne would become to rely on these pills, to keep her figure where it needed to be. Jayne was very good during her pregnancies, she wouldn't smoke or drink, which would become an issue as the years went by.

Jayne came from a long line of drinkers in her blood line, her mother always enjoyed pitchers of manhattans during her daily bridge tournaments, with her lady friends. A ritual handed down from Vera & Helen's mother.

Thanks to the pills and Jayne's determination, the body beautiful was soon back in shape, and Jayne & Mickey performed another engagement at the Tropicana in Las Vegas, after their engagement was held over an additional four weeks at the Tropicana, Bob Hope asked Jayne to perform in his USO tour of Alaska.

Meanwhile back in Hollywood, Fox plotted Jayne's next

couple of movies, and of course, they were to be filmed in England. TOO HOT TO HANDLE (1959) and THE CHALLENGE (1960) were the names of her next endeavors. Of course there was more controversy and scandal over Jayne's costume in TOO HOT a.k.a. PLAYGIRL AFTER DARK.

The original version of the film was shot in color, but upon viewing Jayne's risqué see-through mesh with strategically placed sequins costume, the sequins didn't stay where they were supposed to. Instead of re filming the sequins, the foreign production decided to strip the negatives of the color process to make it black & white, so they could "paint" a white bikini over each frame of her number, wearing the scandalous outfit.

Stills of Jayne in color were printed once again in Playboy, not making anyone happy about it, except her male fans.

Jayne's movie The Challenge, was a serious role, and Jayne played the part of a crime-spree mastermind. She received good reviews in Europe and won a best actress award in England and in France for this movie. Sadly the movie was poorly distributed in the United States, and none of her American fans got to see her above average work.

After filming completed on these two movies Jayne finds out that she is pregnant once again. Jayne & Mickey were already signed to a low budget Italian film, THE LOVES OF HERCULES (1960), a dreadful Hercules movie where Jayne played multiple roles (a Brunette and Red-Headed Queen) in of all things a padded bra. A very restricting corset was designed with metal boning to hide her pregnancy.

The movie was filmed in great parts of Rome and Mickey was in his best physical shape, but the script was the worst, and the special effects even more disappointing than that. Jayne honestly thought that being in Rome, that she was filming another "Cleopatra', but she is soon aware that the second rate movie company was not going to prevail.

Three quarters of the way through filming production shut down on the film, because the Italian film company had used all of their budget. Jayne yelled and screamed on the phone to 20th Century Fox, demanding that they get involved since they contracted her out to do the movie. Fox reluctantly sent money to finish the film and bring home their troubled star.

The next publicity stunt also is still seen today on video, in every mention of Jayne. Jayne was to present at the 1960 Golden Globes Awards. Marilyn Monroe also attended this year, because she was nominated for Best Actress in Some Like It Hot. Jayne knew Marilyn Monroe would be there, so as she did a couple years previous, she picked out a very tight cocktail dress, with spaghetti straps and a plunging neckline.

Of course being in her first trimester, her breasts were very large, and when Ronald Reagan announced Jayne's name to come up to present, she made sure she was in the farthest point of the room, so the cameras would catch every wiggle to the podium. When she announced the winner, in their absence, actor Mickey Rooney accepted the award.

The crowd roared with laughter as tiny Mickey Rooney approached the very exposed Jayne, with the high heels she was wearing, and Mickey Rooney's lack of height, his face was right at breast level. As Jayne saw the crowd reaction, she put her arm around him and pulled him even closer. The crowd roared even loader, Mickey Rooney turned beat red and lost his composure. He stuttered out the words, "Who....ahhh..... Who wants to be tall?".

As he tried to talk more Jayne worked her dress until her right side strap slipped off her shoulder. The crowd roared with laughter, he lost his composure again, and Jayne was the talk of the room, for days after the event.

Marilyn Monroe who was sitting right up front, seemed to enjoy the stunt, she was caught on camera laughing and clapping, so either Marilyn had lots of champagne in her, or she was genuinely entertained.

Jayne once again achieved her goal of being the talk of the town for weeks after the event. Unfortunately none of this juicy publicity helped land her a "good" part in an A-list movie role to help change her image.

After all the hoopla died down, Jayne completed a small role (but received star billing) in "THE GEORGE RAFT

STORY"(1961), she looked really good in her undersized dresses and metal boned corsets. She played the part of Betty Grable, who once romanced George Raft. Even though she got star billing she was only in about 20 minutes of film. This movie was another loan out from Fox to Allied Artists.

It seemed like that's all she was wanted for, the big name, just for window dressing, but the small roles and European productions with small budgets were taking their toll on her career, and the peroxide was taking its toll on her hair.

Jayne had been slowly losing hair since the studio started dying her hair the platinum color in 1957, but by 1960, Jayne had to wear lots of hair pieces and wigs to make up for her thinning hair and broken ends. Jayne basically wore nothing but wigs from 1960 till the end of her life.

CHAPTER SIX
AND BABY MAKES THREE!

Jayne's second son, and third child, Zoltan Anthony is born on August 1, 1960 one month premature but healthy, he weighed in at just 6 pounds.

Mickey and Jayne were elated over their newborn son, and welcomed the TV show, Person to Person into their newly finished Pink Palace, and the newest addition to the family. Jayne & Mickey give a tour of the home with its 20 foot chandelier, heart shaped swimming pool and bathtubs, musical fountains and three inch wall to wall shag carpeting. This was the house that love built.

Not long after giving birth to Zoltan, Jayne was pressed to lose baby weight and fly to Greece to film "IT HAPPENED IN ATHENS" which was released two years later in 1962. The movie was a Fox Picture about the first Olympic Games held in 1896, in Athens. I guess Fox didn't think a movie about the Olympic Games would be a big draw so it seems like they just inserted a part to show off Jayne's Assets.

While filming, Jayne fell for co-star Trax Coltan and had a romantic involvement, while Mickey took care of the children. This was one example of the degree of Mickey's unconditional love for Jayne, he wanted her to be happy, at any cost to him.

Mickey & Jayne recovered from this when filming ended, and went to Las Vegas to appear in another show, HOUSE OF LOVE at the Dunes hotel for $35,000 a week. This show is recorded and released as an LP called, "JAYNE BUSTS UP LAS VEGAS". After this engagement was fulfilled, Jayne & Family appear on "This Is Your Life" and Jayne's parents Harry & Vera Peers also appear, along with Jayne-Marie, Miklos & Zoltan. Jayne is given her Gold charm bracelet that she wore all the time, and was on her wrist when she passed on in 67.

Jayne was then offered a TV guest star role in the TV Program "FOLLOW THE SUN" in 1962 and gets great reviews. Her part was a spoof on the Award winning film Born Yesterday, in the role Judy Holiday made famous. Brian Keith was the male co-star.

After her television guest star role, she was on her way to Europe again, to star with Maurice Chevalier, Mike Connors and Eleanor Parker in the movie "Panic Button", which wasn't released officially for two years after completion in 1964. This was Jayne's last "loan-out" picture under her fox contract, her contract along with many other 20th Century Fox stars was dropped due to the studio nearing bankruptcy from all the delays involved with filming Elizabeth Taylor's Cleopatra.

Jayne was suppose to be filming a scene where she was doing the twist with Maurice Chevalier, when she was notified of her being dropped. I don't know if this sent her into a wild frame of mind, but she really started tying one on, until all hours of the evening.

She had a brief romantic involvement with co-star Mike Connors, before she started a much more serious love affair, with the film's producer Enrico Bomba, who was then still married to his estranged wife.

Jayne had already filed for divorce from Mickey, before leaving for Italy, much to his disbelief. They had a bad argument over him not wanting her to take the children to Italy while filming. Mickey agreed to take the children, but Jayne had still filed the divorce papers.

When filming was completed, Mickey flew home with the children, while Jayne stayed in Italy with Bomba. Later that fall Jayne gets permission from Mickey to Divorce in Mexico, she announces that she will Marry Enrico Bomba. But what really happened was Jayne's drinking was growing worse, and Bomba didn't want to be involved any longer with the troubled blonde and decided to return to his wife.

Jayne went back to Mickey's open arms and everything seemed okay, for now.

CHAPTER SEVEN
SHOCK & DISBELIEF

During this time the shocking news of Marilyn Monroe's tragic death at age 36, that August of 1962, rang out in headlines around the world. Jayne was shocked, saddened and in total disbelief. Even though Monroe acted threatened by Jayne, Jayne had nothing but adoration for her, and felt that things were going to drastically change in Hollywood for all blonde sex symbols, and sadly she was correct.

Its very strange how Marilyn's death affected the industry, and the need for blonde sex symbols. It was like all parts and work for blondes disappeared to honor her. This was another obstacle Jayne had to fight, she had a lot of overhead, and needed to work.

While vacationing in the Bahamas, what was suppose to be a relaxing time turned tense. Jayne & Mickey rented a speedboat to go water skiing, it was a beautiful hot sunny day. After a few runs each skiing, Jayne lost her balance and fell of her skis and disappeared into the water. Mickey jumped in immediately to look for her, but she was know where to be seen. The boat washed up ashore, and the media was alerted. Jayne & Mickey were both missing for two days, and feared to be lost. Headlines made the front page across the country.

Jayne & Mickey were recovered floating in the middle of the ocean, exhausted and both had 3rd degree sunburn. There was a tearful re-union, with Mickey, Jayne and the kids, then Jayne was hospitalized for heatstroke and dehydration.

Many people thought this was one of Jayne's famous publicity stunts gone wrong, but Jayne swore to all that it wasn't.

When Jayne & Mickey returned to the pink palace, it seemed like Jayne's thirst for alcohol had increased, and so did the fighting and the screaming.

Early in 1963, Footage is shot for the Movie, "SPREE" which is a documentary about Las Vegas Lounge Acts, but the movie isn't released until 1967. Jayne & Mickey were filmed doing part of their Vegas night club routine where he lifts her and they do the adagio. Jayne is also filmed doing her, "satire" on the strip.

Jayne & Mickey were offered starring roles in a then controversial movie called PROMISES, PROMISES (1963) with Marie McDonald & Tommy Noonan. It was to be the movie world's first nude scene in a major Hollywood movie, and Jayne's was the candidate.

Mickey was not enthused about Jayne the mother of three, appearing nude in a film, and to make things completely worse, Playboy magazine was covering the shoot and doing a special feature layout called, "THE NUDEST JAYNE MANSFIELD". The movie is soon banned in many cities in the USA. Hugh Hefner is arrested in Chicago for the issue of his world famous magazine being lude & indecent. It was a relatively harmless move by today's standards but back in 1963, not a smart move for an actress who wished to be taken seriously.

I really feel that Jayne's motivation was the paycheck, she received a $150, 000 for the movie and an additional $25, 000 for the Playboy pictorial which to this day, was the only time Hugh Hefner was arrested with anything to do with his publication. It was also the highest selling issue of the magazine to date.

Jayne was very good in Promises, Promises! Funny, witty and very beautiful. Designer Richard Blackwell (the famous Mr. Blackwell), was furious when Jayne used all of the clothing he designed for her in the movie, and gave him screen credit. If the movie hadn't been so controversial, he would have been thrilled. Instead he denounced Jayne, and when he announced his best dress list in 1964, he made a new category for her, " Worst Undressed".

Tommy Noonan claims to have had an affair with Jayne during the filming of the movie, but knowing the kind of man that Jayne was drawn to, and knowing some other lies Tommy Noonan told, I believe he dreamed the whole thing up. Another more serious rumor, and link to Jayne was John F. Kennedy, Paul Blaine (Jayne's Road Manager) and Ray Strait (Jayne's Press Secretary & Biographer) both claim, that Jayne had an affair with President Kennedy, but knowing the two of their reputations, I highly doubt it.

It's really funny how many people claim to have had affairs with famous people, but I always find it very fascinating, how the stars are not around to contest the allegation.

Jayne decides to kick Mickey out once again and starts a passionate affair with Singer Nelson Sardelli. They met at Jayne's first nightclub engagement at the Gus Stevens Supper Club in Biloxi, Mississippi in 1963, (where Jayne was performing when she died).

Jayne files again for divorce in California again, but she cant wait and gets a Mexican Divorce from Mickey, so that she can marry Nelson who is then still married. Jayne announces her divorce from Mickey publicly and also pronounces her love for Nelson. While she is with Nelson, Jayne films two movies in Germany "DOG EAT DOG"(1963) and "HOMESICK FOR ST PAULI" (1963) which Nelson has a cameo.

Jayne is photographed in the pink palace with Nelson, in matching suede fringed jackets, and Jayne introduces Nelson to her entire family, who seems to really like the handsome Brazilian Lounge Singer.

Not much was written about the sudden break-up of Nelson & Jayne, but I really feel that he, like Paul, didn't like living in her shadow. I also feel that her drinking had something to do with it as well. Jayne was not a happy drunk, she flirted and laughed, sometimes yelled and screamed, and pushed the buttons of the people closest to her, to test their devotion to her. I believe that Jayne truly loved Nelson, but he didn't have what it took to survive life with her.

Jayne-Marie Mansfield in 2005, was quoted in an A&E Biography of her late mother, " It was her (Jayne) life, and the rest of us were just along for the ride".

Jayne & Jayne- Marie in Dallas in 1953

Vera & Jayne in Dallas 1944

Jayne at Highland Park High School

Jayne practicing ballet 1947

Jayne & Paul Mansfield's Wedding

Jayne & Jayne Marie 1954

Jayne at 20th Century Fox

Jayne Press Tour in 1957

Jayne & 13 Karat Diamond Ring from Mickey

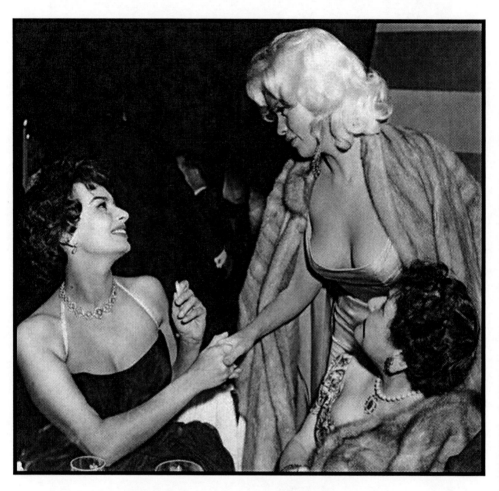

The Famous Night at Romanoff's 1957

Jayne and Stepfather Harry in 1958

Jayne & Mickey's Wedding on Jan 13, 1958

J Jayne in England in 1959

Jayne and Mickey Jr. 1959

Jayne being interviewed 1959

Jayne & Mickey 1960

Jayne in Palm Springs1961

Jayne at Pink Palace 1961

Jayne in Pink Palace Kitchen

Jayne & Mickey Rescued in 1962

Jayne & Mickey in Palm Springs 1961

Jayne & Mickey & Friend 1961

Jayne in 1963

Jaynes Family Christmas Photo 1963

Jayne & Family in Palm Springs

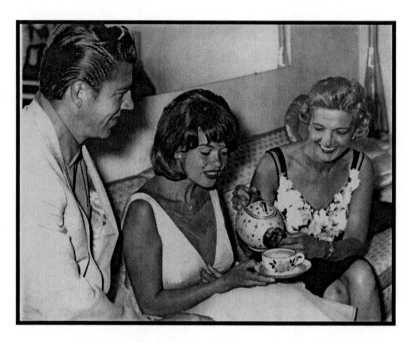

Jayne, Mickey & Aunt Helen in Pen Argyl in 1961

Jayne & Mickey signing autographs in NYC 1966

Baby Mariska Hargitay in 1964

Mariska & Jayne home from the hospital

Jayne, Mickey & Ann B. Davis on stage in "Bus Stop"

Jayne, Mickey, Vera, Mickey Jr. & Jayne- Marie

Jayne with the kids in Biloxi in 1963

Matt & Jayne & Family 1966

Very pregnant with Mariska 1963

The Cimber Family Xmas Card in 1965

Jayne at Whiskey a Go Go 1966

Jayne & Fan backstage 1966

Zoltans's home from Hospital December 1966

Jayne and the kids in April of 1967

Jayne with all her children in 67

Jayne in Vietnam February 1967

Painting of Jayne 1967

Advertisement for Jayne's Final Appearance

Jayne on Stage June 23, 1967

Jayne's last show June 28, 1967

Jayne's Funeral in Pen Argyl 7/3/67

Jayne's Bronze Casket in Hearst 7/3/67

Jayne's Grave in 2006

Jayne's Pink Palace

FRANK FERRUCCIO

"The author and his obsession"

CHAPTER EIGHT
UNCONDITIONAL LOVE

After the Jayne & Nelson split, Jayne decides to reconcile with Mickey and the two of them make a statement to the press about their unconditional love for each other. They do not get re-married because they say that their Mexican divorce is invalid.

During the heat of the reconciliation, Jayne discovers that she is pregnant again. Jayne & Mickey always seemed their happiest when expecting a child, and this pregnancy would be no different. Mickey embraced the idea of being a father again, and he said, " this child will be special, because it will be a recommitment of his and Jayne's love for each other."

On January 23, 1964, Jayne gives birth to her second daughter, Mariska Magdolna Hargitay, named after Mickey's Mother in Hungary. The bliss of a new child didn't last very long, and soon Jayne's drinking and need for diet pills to lose the baby weight, became a struggle for all around her.

I hate making Jayne sound like an alcoholic, because I love who she was, everyone goes through a rough spell in their life, especially when they have reached the peaks of their dreams so early on in life. I feel Jayne's biggest disappointment was not being able to outgrow the dumb blonde image she had instilled in the entertainment world, a parody of an iconic image.

Jayne was human and the highs and lows of a woman who was chronically giving birth and living with flaring hormones, stress and an unfulfilled, unquenchable need for love, would be hard for any one person to bear. She coped how she saw her mother and grandmother cope, and family members alike.

Jayne soon goes back to work and films an episode of the TV show , "BURKE"S LAW". Since the movie offers are slim, she decides to do a Summer Stock production of the play BUS STOP with her playing the lead and Mickey playing the bus driver, rounding out the cast is Ann B Davis (Alice from the Brady Bunch), Stephen Brooks and Elizabeth Hartman. The director of the play is up and coming stage director Matt Cimber.

CHAPTER NINE
THE CIMBER YEARS

J ayne starts hanging out with Matt Cimber a.k.a Matteo Ottaviano, socially, drinking long into the night. Poor Mickey stays at the hotel with the kids. I think that Jayne was inspired by Matt, and his seriousness for the theatre. Jayne Thought that Matt could turn her career around, and finally be taken seriously. So Jayne & Matt fall in "love" while working together, Matt, Jayne, Mickey & the kids fly to Italy so Jayne can film, "PRIMITIVE LOVE"(1964). Mickey again has a small part in the film and also in a documentary about Jayne which isn't released until after her death, called "THE WILD, WILD WORLD OF JAYNE MANSFIELD" (1968).

Mickey & Jayne officially break up again, but do not divorce because they say that her Mexican divorce that she filed a year earlier is valid.

After her quickie foreign films Jayne toured in the play, "GENTLEMEN PREFER BLONDES" to good reviews. Mickey is still hanging out during all of this, and even has a part in the play.

Jayne thought that Matt was going to be her Carlo Ponti, to her Sophia Loren, but in all actuality it turned out to be Jayne's bank account to Matt's parasitic qualities.

After touring for a few months, Jayne & Matt decide that they should get married. So just over the border in Baja, Mexico on September 24, 1964, Matt & Jayne get hitched, and there was nothing pink about it. After arriving home to the Pink Palace, it was decided that they would close up the California mansion, and the whole family, minus Mickey would move to New York City.

I think Matt thought that Jayne had a better chance of being taken serious as an actress in NY, away from the bubble headed blonde image she had instilled in the movie worlds minds in Los Angeles.

Jayne & Matt, (actually Jayne) decide to purchase a Park Ave & E 69th Street Townhouse. It is right around the block from the Italian Consulate. Jayne keeps the pink palace, but has the house closed up, and has her prized belongings and her Bentley Convertible shipped to New York, as well as all the children's toys & stuff.

Matt has Jayne on a rigorous schedule, Jayne stars in a play which Matt directed called, "The Champagne Complex". She also briefly returns to Hollywood to film a cameo for MGM's "THE LOVED ONE" (1965), but unfortunately is cut from the final edit of the film.

During her time in New York, Jayne appears on numerous game shows filmed in New York. Jayne appeared on Down you Go!, Password, The Match Game and What's My Line? She also stars in a Dramatic film which is filmed over the next year and a half called, "SINGLE ROOM FURNISHED". She plays three different characters in the released version of the film, but it was unfinished when Jayne passed away, so Matt decided to cash in on her demise and piece what he had together with an added storyline, and released it in 1968.

During this time Jayne intentionally or not, makes headlines again. Mickey Hargitay & Matt Cimber are photographed hitting each other while Jayne screams and Mickey Jr & Zoltan cry. These photos show up all over the country, of the two men fighting for Jayne's love and honor. Or is it Just another publicity stunt?

Jayne announces she will have her fifth child in October of

1965, But still has time to make a horrible little movie in Florida called, "THE FAT SPY" (1965) starring Phyllis Diller. The movie also starred Jack E. Leonard and Brian Donlevy. Jayne is visibly pregnant in the movie which is a take off on 1960's beach movies. The script is horrible and you can see the low budget in each frame of the movie.

When Jayne returns home to NY, she finds that her townhouse is broken into and $51,000 in jewelry is stolen. Jayne gives birth to her fifth child Antonio Raphael Ottaviano a.k.a Anthony Richard Cimber on October 17, 1965 in California.

After little Tony was born, Jayne's drinking grew bad again, and she was starving herself and taking amphetamines to lose the baby weight. Jayne does a quickie starring cameo in "LAS VEGAS HILLBILLYS" (1965) with Mamie Van Doren, her chief competition and rival.

Jayne never seemed very enthused by Mamie's presence, but still being overweight from childbirth, she refused to be in their one scene in the movie together. Instead the scene was filmed using a body double in a blonde wig, Mamie has been interviewed as saying, she didn't have any idea why.

Jayne is quickly back to work in another of Matt's plays called, "THE RABBIT HABIT". It was a huge disappointment, but Jayne managed to score a big hit in the middle of winter in 1965 at the LATIN QUARTER in New York. She played to a sold out house for two months, and also does her last filming for Single Room Furnished.

Jayne is very thin and is acting very flighty, Jayne and Matt are not getting along at all at this point. Jayne is hanging out drinking with Matt's cousin Greg Tyler, who states in his book that him and Jayne had a tumultuous affair right in front of Matt's eyes. I highly doubt that any of this is true, after seeing him stand & model in every clip I managed to see him in. He admits to being a male hustler in his book, which I do believe, but I believe, only for homosexual men.

Nonetheless, Matt is disturbed by her drinking and staying out late with Greg, and I'm not really sure that it is intentional or not, but Matt starts spending a little too much time with Jayne-Marie, who is developing into a voluptuous woman herself at the age of fifteen.

Jayne & Matt enjoyed playing cat & mouse with each other, purposely doing things to annoy the other. Jayne was not a victim in any sense of the word, and knew how to get to people. Matt was a hotheaded Italian, and was raised in the manner that it was okay to hit a woman. So Jayne & Matt had some real knockout fights with each other, and what started out as a fun relationship, later turned to hate.

Jayne started another run of Gentlemen Prefer Blondes in stock in 1966 with Matt directing. Jayne looked flawless and thin, but the madness of pills and booze were starting to take its toll on the aging sexy blonde.

Jayne surprises everyone when she announces on the Mike Douglas Show, that her & Matt are separated. I really don't know the facts behind the separation, whether it was her jealousy over the time & attention he was giving Jayne-Marie, or if it was the constant fighting and bruising. Matt knew that Jayne was very insecure about her age and her appearance, and purposely doted over Jayne-Marie to make Jayne even more insecure.

During this turbulent time, Jayne called Mickey who was then filming a movie in Italy, and asked him to come to her side, their were rumors of reconciliation for them, but the rumors were just that.

I think that Jayne & Mickey had an undying love for each other, and when the tension was taken off the table, the two of them loved each others company. Mickey was happy to see the children, but Jayne's drinking and behavior was too much for Mickey to witness, so back to Italy he went, where he was having his own success in the movie business.

CHAPTER TEN
JAYNE ACTS OUT IN 1966

While still in New York, Jayne met and fancied a writer by the name of Jan Cremer. He wrote a best seller that was self titled, "I, Jan Cremer'. Jayne started a brief love affair with him and actually decided to take him along with her and her Venezuela night club tour.

Even though Jayne really didn't love Matt, she still took the break up of her marriage hard, and found another reason to party and forget about all of it. Jayne signed legal separation papers before leaving, and left the kids in care of Jayne Marie and her maid Linda.

Ted Sifo was Jayne's tour manager, and was warned by Matt, who was still managing her career, that she was going to be a handful.

When Jayne arrived in Venezuela, she was greeted by hundreds of people (mainly men), who were yelling and chanting her name. She was escorted to her hotel and brought to her guest suite, where she was greeted by the hotel manager and food & champagne.

Jayne loved the star treatment, she told Ted, " I love it here, I may never leave."

In the latter days, anyplace that Jayne got the star treatment, was her favorite place and she didn't want to leave. She met a very attractive young man at one of the nightclubs that she was working in, his name was Douglas Olivares. Douglas said he was 18, but I believe that he was a little younger.

Jayne was overtaken by his good looks, and instantly wanted him to work for her, as her bodyguard, which was ridiculous since, he was a tiny guy. I believe that Jayne fed off of the relationship with Douglas that he was so beautiful in her eyes, and young and full of life. The romance with Jan Cremer was finished and now it was Douglas.

During this whole time, Matt was still managing Jayne's career, so there were calls back and fourth to the USA, screaming, throwing things in Matt's face, especially the romance with Douglas. Matt seemed unaffected, all he was concerned with was getting custody of Tony.

When Jayne arrived back in Los Angeles, she still had Douglas with her, and planned on taking him to Las Vegas where she was booked to appear in the beginning of September at The Freemont Hotel.

Jayne's act at the Freemont, was a lot less lavish than her past engagements there with Mickey. Jayne was a true professional, on time to rehearse, knew her songs, always on time. During this period, she sang, songs like Embrace Me, Promise her Anything, and Strangers in the night, while she did her usual, sitting and singing on the laps of men in the audience.

Jayne's after show antics, were something less than professional, staying out till all hours of the night, hitting all the hot spots with Douglas.

After returning home to the pink palace, Jayne noticed that Douglas was spending too much time, with Jayne-Marie, so she made arrangements for him to go back to Venezuela.

CHAPTER ELEVEN
THE DIVORCE LAWYER

Jayne decides that its time to take care of unfinished business, and divorce Matt. She knows that to win full custody of Tony, she will need a really strong attorney. At the law firm of Melvin Belli, which was a very prominent firm at that time, representing Jimmy Hoffa, was a very good looking but short man named Samuel Brody.

Sam Brody was married and had two children, his wife was in a wheelchair, because she had multiple sclerosis. When Jayne and Sam first met, there was electricity in the air, each having a strong attraction for the other.

Jayne started calling Sam at home to ask him legal questions, and his wife Beverly was not happy about it all. I'm sure that Sam's marriage had taken on a more companion like quality, because of his wife's illness, so I really feel that the flirtation of a still very beautiful & voluptuous movie star, was just much too much for him to resist.

Soon Sam and Jayne embark in a full fledged love affair. Night after night, Beverly Brody would call the pink palace looking for her husband, but he was always too busy to come to the phone.

The last straw for Sam's wife, was when he spent all of their joint savings on a 20 karat diamond bracelet for Jayne.

Beverly Brody kicked her husband out, and Sam instantly moved into the pink palace with Jayne & family. She filed divorce papers almost immediately, and named Jayne as the adulteress.

The worst part of the relationship with Sam, was that they both had an unquenchable thirst for alcohol. At this point, Jayne & Sam were quickly being labeled at all the Hollywood hot spots as trouble.

Jayne would never let a man get the best of her in a conversation, or let herself be put down in anyway. She was a very strong and intelligent woman, and stood up for herself consistently. The end result of this was many disagreements with Sam, and a consistent power struggle, which resulted in public screaming and fighting.

While all of this was going on Sam was fighting as her lawyer to win full custody of Tony Cimber. Matt was trying to win full custody himself on the claims that Jayne was an unfit mother, at this stage in her life.

Jayne would do anything to make sure that she would not lose one of her children, she would protect them just as a bear would protect their baby cubs.

Jayne even asked her good friend Bob Hope, to write a statement saying what a good mother she was. The court awarded custody of Anthony Cimber to Jayne, but made provisions for Matt to have regular visitation.

With Sam proving himself to Jayne by winning custody for her, she now lets him manage her career. Jayne always would revert back to publicity when she felt her career was in a slump, or there weren't many offers coming in.

So she agreed to Pose for pictures at a southern California attraction called Jungle land. During the photo shoot, Zoltan wondered away from Sam & Jayne, and was no where to be found. He managed to slip through the bars of the Lions Den, and when Jayne realized it, he was already being thrashed about in the mouth of one of the animals.

Jayne screamed, then fainted, while all the workers in the park, tried to contain the lion. Once tranquilized, the lion let go and Zoltan just laid there on the ground lifeless. He was rushed with Jayne by his side to nearest hospital, where he had to have emergency surgery.

Jayne called Mickey in Rome, to come home immediately. The lion had punctured his spleen, and he was bleeding internally. With Jayne And Mickey by little Zoltan's side, he laid there lifeless in a coma.

It looked for a while that they might lose him, Jayne was devastated with grief and guilt over not watching him closely enough. Zoltan experienced many complications during his stay in the hospital, but was well enough to come home for Christmas of 1966, which was another huge press blitz.

During the month of December, Jayne returned for a guest appearance in her first Hollywood movie in years for 20th Century Fox. The film "A GUIDE FOR THE MARRIED MAN" (1967), was being directed by Gene Kelly, and they were using big stars to illustrate cinereous of how not to get caught cheating on your wife.

It was actually an honor for Jayne to return to the studio, in which she had started, sadly this was Jayne's last appearance in a movie.

CHAPTER TWELVE
1967 AND DEATH

I am sure that no one could have imagined that 1967 would become Jayne's last year of life, or maybe they did. Jayne didn't talk to Mickey or Harry & Vera Peers, much at all in 67. I have watched interviews with Mickey in current day, and he said that they were all waiting for something terrible to happen, but I don't think anyone thought it would be this.

Jayne's looks were starting to show that her life was anything but heaven. She looked very puffy and bloated, her drinking has accelerated into alcoholic proportions and no one can get through to her about it.

Sam had arranged a tour of British nightclubs, she took Sam & Tony with her.

The other children stayed with Mickey. Jayne was bruised and bloated in too tight mini-dresses with Go-Go Boots sitting on gentlemen's laps in the audience. Jayne & Sam drank and fought nightly, and photos were printed of the two of them beating on each other. It was a very sad scene for a woman who had been the most photographed woman in the world ten years earlier.

The timing was really off for Jayne, meeting Sam, when her addictions were peeking was very unfortunate. Sam was a controller, he didn't want anyone that was close to Jayne previously talking to her at all. This included, Mickey, Jayne-Marie and her parents and other relatives.

Jayne-Marie had taken over for her mother in her years of decline, she became nursemaid, hairdresser, baby-sitter, surrogate mother to her siblings as well as counselor. As Jayne's drinking grew worse, so did her relationship with Jayne-Marie who really was her best friend, more than her daughter. Jayne & Sam's relationship was so dangerous and violent, Jayne-Marie couldn't take it anymore.

One night after a bad fight with Jayne, Sam turned on Jayne-Marie with a belt, and this was the final straw for the young girl. Jayne-Marie fled the pink palace with just one suitcase of clothing, and one pair of borrowed high heel shoes that belonged to her mother.

She went to stay with her Aunt, Paul Mansfield's sister and when they saw the bruises on the girl, they called the police. Jayne & Sam were taken to court over the incident, Jayne-Marie stated that the house was not a safe environment for any of the children, and thought they needed to be taken away from Jayne's custody.

Jayne and Sam had to show in court on June 20, but the case was issued a continuance until Jayne fulfilled a nightclub engagement in Biloxi, Mississippi at Gus Stevens Supper Club.

Sam got into a car accident in the red Ferrari that Jayne had bought for him, pulling out of the front gates of the pink palace on June 21st, and broke his leg, which had to be cast. Anton La Vey, an actor, and leader of the church of Satan, has claimed that he put a curse on Sam, and this is why the accident happened. He also had supposedly warned Jayne to stay away from Sam, because he would die before the year was out.

Jayne's appearance in photos with Anton La Vey was nothing more than a publicity scheme. Jayne did not practice black magic, or follow any of the "Churches of Satan", I hate that all of this is always played up in the press, and in 'stories" still told today by La Vey's daughter.

Jayne & Sam (with his leg freshly cast) took Mickey Jr., Zoltan & Mariska & 3 Chihuahuas to Biloxi, Mississippi with them. Jayne wanted to take Tony but Matt got an injunction so that she couldn't leave the state with him. They flew into Keesler Air Force Base in Biloxi, Mississippi so that they could tour the base and Jayne could visit the wounded soldiers back from Vietnam on the base.

Jayne was set to perform from June 24th- June 29th, a gig that was switched with Mamie Van Doren, when Mamie couldn't fulfill the engagement. Mamie has always felt guilt over this, that if they hadn't switched performance dates, that Jayne would still be with us. I truly believe that you cannot alter destiny, and it was her fate to go at this time.

Jayne, Sam & Family flew in on the 23rd of June, and while being driven to the Edgewater Gulf Hotel in Biloxi, Jayne & Sam saw a yellow Rolls Royce at a car lot. They purchased the Rolls Royce together, and paid for it with a check. Jayne drives since Sam's leg is in a cast and can't.

The week in Biloxi started out like a much needed vacation for the family. Jayne made the local publicity rounds touring the area.

Jayne starts her gig at Gus Stevens' Club, she does three shows a night 7:30, 9:30, 11:30, she sings Strangers In the Night, Promise Her Anything, Embrace Me, and assorted others each night. She is in good spirits and enjoys being away.

Jayne has an interview scheduled for an early morning talk show in New Orleans for the 29th, so the plan is that they will drive the Rolls Royce to New Orleans after her last show at the supper club on the 28th. It is about a two hour ride along old highway 90.

During the day of the 28th, Jayne , Sam and family tour Keesler Air Force base, and pictures are taken for the local paper, of Jayne posing with soldiers in the base hospital. Later that night, the Rolls Royce that Jayne & Sam purchased was repossessed in the parking lot of the Hotel by the car lot owner, because the check that they gave him had bounced.

Jayne & Sam were very upset and asked Gus Stevens to hire them a limousine to drive them all to New Orleans after her last show.

Gus didn't want to foot the expense, (the biggest mistake in Gus Stevens' life), so he said that they could take his wife's car, it was a big 1966 Buick Electra 225 four door sedan. It had just been checked out by the Car dealer and it was fine. Sam asked him to find someone who could drive them there, since his foot was in a cast and he didn't want Jayne to have to drive that late at night.

Gus Stevens asked Ronnie Harrison, an employee of the club, and his daughters fiancé to drive them in the Buick and then come back to Biloxi the same night. Ronnie worked at the Naval Base as a security guard and had just gotten off a double shift. Gus told him to go home and sleep for a few hours and come back to the club around midnight to drive them, he agreed.

Jayne's last show was a good one, I interviewed a lady who had seen Jayne's 11:30 show on the 28th. She was a friend of Gus's and had a drink with Jayne & Sam after the show. She said that Jayne was in really good spirits and was very coherent.

At around 12 midnight Ronnie returned to the club to drive the troop to New Orleans, Gus had removed the interior dome lights from the Buick because he knew that Jayne liked to paste pictures in her scrapbook while traveling and didn't want the lights to distract the overtired Ronnie.

The Buick was loaded with all the luggage, the dog cages, the three children , three dogs and three adults. It was around 12:30 a.m. when they set off on their last ride. Jayne asked Ronnie to stop at a gas station to see if they could fix the lights on the inside of the car.

As predicted by Gus Stevens, Jayne wanted to paste some clippings in her scrapbook which was in her big white tote bag. The attendants at the station didn't have the right size bulbs so they set off down highway 90.

Ronnie and Sam were in the front seat with Zoltan holding two dogs, Jayne, Mariska, and Mickey Jr. in the back with the other three. It was a hot, humid night in June, there was a heavy mist in the air. On Highway 90 in Slidell, Louisiana about 45 minutes from New Orleans was an all-night restaurant called "THE

WHITE KITCHEN".

According to a witness Jayne & family had pulled up in front of the restaurant around 2:00 am, only Jayne exited the car, and entered the restaurant. She asked one of the waitresses where, "the little Girls room was".

After exiting the bathroom, Jayne stopped at the counter and asked for some cookies and some coke's. A lady and her son sitting at a nearby booth, asked if she was Jayne Mansfield, and Jayne replied, "The One And Only". The lady asked what she was doing in the middle of Louisiana in the middle of the night, Jayne said she had been performing on the Biloxi coast and was on her way to New Orleans for an early morning talk show on WDSU-TV Channel 6. The lady and her son, got Jayne's autograph (the last autograph).

Jayne said good night to the lady and her son and left the restaurant, they watched Jayne from the window. Jayne moved the sleeping Zoltan from the front seat and put him in the backseat with his already sleeping brother & sister. Jayne sat by the passenger window with a dog on her lap. This was the last time Jayne was seen alive, she was about ten miles away from her impending doom.

From witness statements in the official police report, the Buick flew past several cars on highway 90 doing around 80 miles an hour. A mosquito spraying pesticide machine had just sprayed the marsh land by the Rigolets bridge, directly where they were headed.

A very slow moving tractor trailer driven by Richard Rambo of Pensacola, Florida was creeping through the fog of the machine. Mr. Rambo knew this road well and knew that the steel girder bridge was coming up soon. He was driving about 25 miles an hour, when he felt a jarring impact from the rear and immediately stopped to see what had hit him.

Upon walking to the rear of the truck, Mr. Rambo saw what looked like a steaming smashed convertible. Smoke was coming from under the hood of the car, and heard crying coming from the rear of the car. The truck driver, in a state of shock, thought the car might catch fire, so he decided to get everyone out of the car.

He first tried to open the rear passenger door, but it wouldn't open. He did manage to open the passenger front door where Jayne was sitting. He removed Jayne's lifeless body from the passenger seat, he could see she was visibly dead because about a half an inch above her eyebrows back was gone, and laid her down on the shelled shoulder of the roadway.

By this time the two vehicles that the speeding Buick had passed on the highway had stopped to see if they could help. The gentlemen and woman from both cars helped the truck driver pry the back door open and remove two crying little boys (Mickey Jr. & Zoltan), two little Chihuahuas jumped from the back seat as well. One of the little boys (Zoltan) was screaming, "my sister, my sister!!!!"

Upon further investigating, the men saw some movement from behind the front seat, under the luggage which had traveled from the trunk on top of the back seat area from the impact. Mariska's head was stuck between the front seat and the metal pillar of the car, she was bleeding badly.

One of the people from the cars ran to the home across the street from where the accident had occurred and knocked on the door. The door immediately opened and the woman said there was a terrible accident at the end of their drive.

The people in the house were awoken by the sound of the crash and had already called the police, who had just arrived at the scene. The two officers ran to the car to see if they could help free the girl, they used a tire iron to pry the seat loose and free the little girl who had a very deep laceration on the side of her face.

The lady and gentlemen who stopped volunteered to drive the children to the hospital which was about 10 miles away, so they left with Mariska, Zoltan and Mickey Jr.

About a half an hour later every police officer in the area was at the scene, it wasn't until investigation of Jayne's bag that they knew it was Jayne Mansfield lying on the side of the road, she was just 34 years old.

API & UPI press as well as local newsman were called, and told that famous Hollywood Sex Symbol Jayne Mansfield had been killed in a horrible car accident.

The county morgue car arrived and the bodies of Sam Brody & Ronnie Harrison were removed from the vehicle. An additional car was called to take them to the morgue. Both Ronnie & Sam's heads were badly smashed into the dashboard, Jayne's head injuries were much higher up on her head, almost as if she tried to duck out of the way of the impending crash.

Vera & Harry Peers, Mickey Hargitay and Matt Cimber were all called in the middle of the night to be told the horrible news. Mickey was told that all 3 children had been hurt and that they were going to fly Mariska by Helicopter to a better equipped hospital in New Orleans for emergency plastic surgery.

Mickey dropped everything and immediately flew to New Orleans to be with the children. Harry & Vera Peers immediately headed for New Orleans as well. Matt Cimber headed to the Pink Palace immediately to take Tony, who thank god had not been in the car. Little Tony most likely would have been in the arms of Jayne.

Two of the three dogs had survived and had been taken to the ASPCA. The next few days were chaos for all involved, There was a huge fight over Jayne's body, very similar to the recent fight and drama over Playmate Anna Nicole Smith's body.

Matt Cimber was legal widower but was being fought by Jayne's parent's and Mickey for custody of Jayne's body. Matt told the Peer's and Mickey that he wanted Jayne buried in California at Forest Lawn with all of the other big stars.

Both the Peers and Mickey said that Jayne wanted to buried in the family plot, in Pen Argyl, PA. next to her grandparents and father.

A Louisiana judge ruled Mickey legal widower because Jayne & Mickey's 1963 Mexican divorce & Matt & Jayne's marriage was not recognized.

A California Judge ruled Matt Cimber legal widower and heir. In the end the Peer's and Mickey won and Jayne would be buried in Pen Argyl, Pennsylvania. Jayne's body was taken from the morgue and brought to Bultman's Funeral home in New Orleans.

Undertaker Jim Roberts spent about 8 hours reconstructing

Jayne's head with body clay, wigs and tons of make-up to have an open casket service. Vera Peers had picked out a lovely pink chiffon high neck ruffled trim dress with matching bow for her hair, for Jayne to be laid out in. Mickey was the only one allowed to see her.

The bronze casket picked out by Mickey was locked and taken to the Airport to be flown into JFK AIRPORT, and then driven to Pen Argyl by the Funeral home. The casket arrived at the Funeral home in Pen Aryl and Harry & Vera Peers & Mickey wanted to see her before anyone else.

There was only one problem the casket had been locked in New Orleans and the key was gone. Vera Pleaded with Undertaker Nick Ruggiero to pry it open, but was talked out of it by Mickey. It was to be a small family service.

The National guard had to fly into Easton, PA to hold back the crowd of nearly 10,000 people lined up to see all the celebrities they thought would be there. It was never confirmed what celebrities did attend, it was rumored that Bob Hope and Zsa, Zsa Gabor attended but this could not be confirmed.

Besides all of Jayne's area cousins and Aunt's & Uncle's, the only immediately family members in attendance were Harry & Vera Peers, Mickey Hargitay, and the only one of Jayne's children to attend was Jayne Marie Mansfield. The children who were in the car were in the hospital in New Orleans and Tony was with Matt Cimber who thought it was best, because of potential conflict not to attend.

It was a huge circus of publicity, a last farewell that Jayne would have loved, she was the Star again, for one last time.

CHAPTER THIRTEEN
THE AFTERMATH

This part of my book I feel is the saddest, but isn't it true how horrible life can be at times.

Jayne was only 34 years old at the time of her death, she lived her life to the fullest every day, never thinking of how it would end. This must be the reason that she did not have a Last Will & Testament. Sadly for her children more than anyone, the lawyers took over, and no one would try to settle anything in best interest of the children.

Marilyn Monroe, 20th Century Fox's biggest star, who made million s of dollars for the studio, died in 1962, with only approximately $150, 000 in the bank. Jayne who was always hailed as "the second class Monroe wannabe" died in 1967, with an estate worth of almost 2 million dollars.

Sadly, she was legally married to both Matt Cimber & Mickey Hargitay when she passed on. Her Mexican divorce was never filed in the USA, so she was still married to Mickey, and she married Matt in Mexico in 1964. Matt & Mickey, never got along, and fought tooth and nail to the end, for title of Jayne's estate.

Since their was no will, the judge in California ruled that all of her possession would be sold, and put in a probate account. All five of Jayne's children left the house, with just their clothes. An Itemized report of all of her belongings was taken the day after she died, by Ray Strait (Jayne's secretary), Linda Murdoch (Jayne's Housekeeper) and two Bel Air Police Officers.

A poorly advertised Estate sale was held in 1967, all of Jayne's belongings that were not sold, stayed with the home. At first the home was rented, and later in 1968, it was sold, for $125, 000 to a retired burlesque star and her Reno, Nevada casino owning husband, Rita & Harry Greenlin..

The house was sold with 273 items of personal items (clothing, jewelry, shoes, furniture, etc). Rita "Simone" Greenlin, sold the house in 1976 to Engelbert Humperdink for $276, 000, except when she left, she took all of Jayne's personal items and kept them for a legacy to her children and grandchildren. The only items that went with the house were Jayne's off white piano with the gold painted cherubs, and pink tufted velvet piano bench, her pink mirrored headboard and the red tufted leather desk and credenza, all made for her by Mickey Hargitay.

Lawsuits went on for years, and wasn't settled until ten years later, in 1977, leaving the estate insolvent. All of the lawyers ate up the estate, Mickey waived a small settlement in favor of the children, so Jayne's five children wound end up with $1100 each, and no personal items to remember their famous mother by.

The saddest part of the whole story for me, I just found out about a year ago. Upon talking to my friend Stephen Ruggiero, the owner of the funeral home in Pen Argyl, Pa where Jayne's funeral was held, I was told that Nick Guerro, the former owner of the funeral home didn't get paid for the Mansfield funeral until almost a year and a half after her death, and you know who paid for it? Jayne's Estate.

CHAPTER FOURTEEN
LIFE GOES ON

I have been more fortunate than most of Jayne's loyal fans, I have had the opportunity to meet and talk with the family of Jayne Mansfield. When you love a celebrity that has passed on, you cant get any closer to them, than being a friend of the family.

I have loyally taken care of Jayne's grave for the past 28 years, always making sure that she had some kind of flower tribute. I even purchased the concrete flower planters that sit on either side of her huge heart shaped marker.

Because I have done this, I have been embraced by the Mansfield children, and know them all.

I have unselfishly given each of them many pictures through the years of their famous mother, some with each child. I have given all of them personal belongings of Jayne's I have purchased through the years, so that each child would have something personal of their mother.

Jayne Marie Mansfield, who is the walking book of Mansfield, has told me many wonderful & sad things about her mother. Jayne Marie is the authority who knew her the best, she was 16 years old when Jayne past on. She is a stunningly beautiful woman, the one in the family I feel looks the most like Jayne, and has the figure of her mom.

Jayne-Marie posed for Playboy herself in 1976, put herself through college and lives in California as a financial advisor, she has one son, and two grandchildren, she has been married once, and has a boyfriend of many years.

Miklos Hargitay lives in Hollywood, and has owned a successful plant shop in town for many years. Mickey Jr. has been married twice and has one son Miklos the third. He is a very handsome man, with big blue eyes, and a very kind soul.

Zoltan Hargitay is married with two beautiful sons, he has been a jack of all trades, but has focused his skill in construction and carpentry, taught to him by his famous father Mickey Hargitay. Zoltan is very angelic, kind, loving and genuine.

Mariska Hargitay is probably the most well know of the family. She has been in the entertainment industry since 1982, she has appeared in many movies, as well as television shows. She is an award winning actress (Golden Globe & Emmy) for her role as Olivia Benson on Law & Order SVU. Mariska is a stunning beauty, who is married to actor Peter Hermann, and recently gave birth to her son August. She has achieved a new level of celebrity, speaking for causes of violence against women, starting her own "Joyful Heart Foundation" and truly giving her all on her show each week. Mariska's talent still blows me away, she is a master of the acting craft, and her mother would have been proud.

Anthony Cimber has worked for many years with his father director Matt Cimber on many entertainment projects. He has acted, produced and directed, as well as worked behind the scenes. He has been married once and has a beautiful little girl, who amazing looks a lot like Jayne. Tony is a very handsome and well spoken man, and I believe has the best qualities of his parents.

Matt Cimber still directs today, he has been married twice since Jayne, and has another son from his second marriage.

Vera & Harry Peers both past away in the latter 1990's, Harry was 81, Vera lived to the age of 97. They are buried next to Jayne in the family plot, with her grandparents, The Palmers & The Jeffrey's, and Jayne's father Herbert, as well as Jayne's mothers sister Helen Manheim.

I must thank the memory of Helen Milheim, for she is the first member of Jayne's family I had the privilege of meeting, and because of, was introduced to the rest of her family.

This book is written with a lot of love and devotion to Jayne Mansfield's memory. Her image and work that she has left behind, has brought me great joy my entire life. There have been so many books written about Marilyn Monroe, and only a few about Jayne. Jayne Mansfield is worthy of the level of tribute that Marilyn still gets today. Jayne was not an imitator, I feel she was a successor.

ACKNOWLEDGEMENTS

I wish to thank my mother & father, Frank & Ellen Ferruccio, for supporting me in my life and goals. My brother Anthony Ferruccio, for taking me to Jayne Mansfield's grave for the first time, my sister Rita Brown, for buying me books with Jayne Mansfield in them.

My life partner John Sweeney, for his consistent love & encouragement, in all of my interests, I love you dearly.

To all of my friends, who are my family, thank you for all of the patience and tolerance with my Jayne madness.

And last but certainly not least, Jayne-Marie, Mickey, Zoltan, Mariska & Tony for allowing me into your lives, and giving me a small glimpse of how wonderful your mother really was, I am forever indebted.

Printed in the United States
83838LV00006B/148-186/A